Secret Codes

Ken Beatty

Level 4

Series Editors: Andy Hopkins and Jocelyn Potter

Pearson Education Limited
Edinburgh Gate, Harlow,
Essex CM20 2JE, England
and Associated Companies throughout the world.

Pack ISBN: 978-1-4058-5222-7
Book ISBN: 978-1-4058-5087-2
CD-ROM ISBN: 978-1-4058-5088-9

This edition first published by Pearson Education Ltd 2007

1 3 5 7 9 10 8 6 4 2

Text copyright © Ken Beatty 2007
Illustrations by Cristián Werb

Set in 11/13pt A. Garamond
Printed in China
SWTC/01

Produced for the Publishers by AC Estudio Editorial S.L.

Published by Pearson Education Ltd in association with Penguin Books Ltd,
both companies being subsidiaries of Pearson Plc

Acknowledgements
We are grateful to the following for permission to reproduce photographs:

Beinecke Rare book and Manuscript Library, Yale University: page 22 (b) (The Voynich Manuscript);
Corbis: page 2 (Tim Wright), page 13 (t) & page 15 (l) (Archivo Iconografico,S.A), page 13 (b)
& page 15 (r) (Gustavo Tomsich), page 65 (© Araldo de Luca), page 68 (© Charles & Josette Lenars), page 70
(© Ashley Cooper); **Getty Images**: page 36 (bl) (News / Tim Boyle), (br) (Neo Vision / Shinya Sasaki),
page 45, page 47 (Hulton Archive), page 53 (Hulton Archive), page 61 (Bridgeman Art Library), page 63;
Photos 12: page 42 (Collection Cinéma); **PunchStock Royalty Free Images**: page 36 (bm)
(Photodisc), (tr) (mixa); **Topfoto**: 61(r); **Wikipedia**: page 22 (t) (The Beale Papers)

Picture research by Natasha Jones

For a complete list of the titles available in the Penguin Active Reading series please write to your local
Pearson Longman office or to: Penguin Readers Marketing Department, Pearson Education,
Edinburgh Gate, Harlow, Essex CM20 2JE, England.

Contents

1.1 What's the book about?

These are discussed in this book. What are they? What do you know about them?

What do you know?

1.2 Write in the boxes below.

Who uses secret codes?	Why do they use them?
soldiers	to keep war secrets from other soldiers

CHAPTER 1

Codes for Life

*The most common codes and ciphers are in your
wallet and they are used every day.*

D o you use secret **codes**? Do you look for and understand strange **symbols**? Do you send and receive messages that only a few other people can understand?

You are probably not a spy, but you certainly use a great number of secret codes, **ciphers**, symbols and messages. Everyone does! For example, which of these symbols makes you think of the word *stop*?

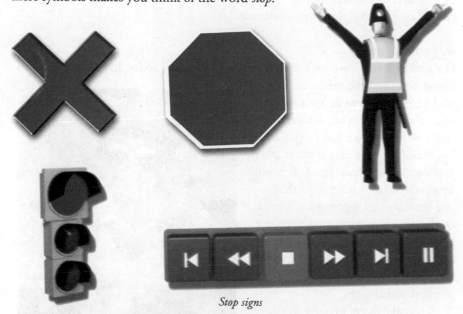

Stop signs

Most of these symbols for *stop* are familiar around the world, but some symbols have different meanings for different people. The colour red might mean *stop* or *danger* to some people, but in China it often means *let's celebrate*.

code /kəʊd/ (n) words, letters or signs that are used together, instead of ordinary writing or speech, to send secret messages. A *bar code* is a number of black lines on a product that can be read by a computer. If you *break a code* or *decode* a secret message, you discover its meaning.
symbol /'sɪmbəl/ (n) a sign (for example, a picture) for a quality, idea or organisation
cipher /'saɪfə/ (n) a method of changing the letters of words with other letters, numbers or symbols to make a secret message. If you *decipher* a message, you *break the cipher* and find the hidden message.

1

Symbols for ideas like *stop* are not meant to be secret. Many codes are just shorter or faster ways of explaining other ideas. A stop sign really says, 'Please wait here for a moment and look around. Are you sure there are no other cars or people that might cause you to have an accident?' It would take too long to read all this at every corner.

Even language is a code. Although you can read the words in this book, you probably could not understand a common word like *stop* in more than a few languages. Other languages might look like secret codes to you. On the other hand, you may use or invent a new language that older people do not understand. Do you understand the word codes in **text** messaging? For example, do you understand this message? GR8 2 C U * This is not meant to be secret code, but many people do not understand it.

● Personal codes

Only your close friends may understand your personal codes, like hand signs, lesson notes and the special meanings of the clothes you wear. Your clothes often show that you are in a certain mood or belong to a certain group. For example, what does it mean when you wear a T-shirt and jeans? It could be a code to tell other people that you are relaxed. Uniforms are formal clothes that give information about a person's school or job. Among soldiers, a uniform and its decorations give a lot of information about the soldier's position and abilities.

A child in uniform

A mistake in your choice of clothes is usually just embarrassing, but sometimes it is dangerous. A few years ago, **gang** members killed a young man in Los Angeles while he walked in the wrong part of the city wearing a red jacket. Red was the colour of another gang. Each gang painted symbols on local buildings to mark their space. This was another kind of code, but the young man probably could not understand their meaning or the danger he was in.

* GR8 2 C U: Great to see you.

text /tekst/ (n) the writing in a book or magazine (not the pictures)
gang /gæŋ/ (n) a group of people, especially trouble-makers or criminals

● Money and prices

But the most common codes and ciphers are in your wallet and they are used every day. Most paper money and bankcards include one or more code numbers to try to stop people printing or stealing money.

Secret codes are also used on almost everything you buy. Bar codes can be read by computer; they give information about the product, including its name and how much it costs. Two shops can use the same bar code on the same product, but decide to price it differently.

A bar code

Long before computers, though, there were other ways to hide information about prices. Shop managers sometimes used an easy-to-remember ten-letter word like *background* to write the cost of products. The letters in *background* **represented** the numbers *zero* to *nine*.

b	a	c	k	g	r	o	u	n	d
0	1	2	3	4	5	6	7	8	9

For example, the manager of a carpet shop could write the four letters *urad* on a carpet to show that it cost him £75.19. When a customer came into the shop, the manager could look at the code and start to discuss the price. The shop manager knew exactly what he could afford to charge.

● Simple ciphers

Each letter or symbol in a simple cipher represents a different letter. In the simplest cipher, each of the twenty-six letters in the English **alphabet** represents a different letter, like the next letter. In this example, the letters are listed from the last to the first.

a	b	c	d	e	f	g	h	i	j	k	l	m
z	y	x	w	v	u	t	s	r	q	p	o	n
n	o	p	q	r	s	t	u	v	w	x	y	z
m	l	k	j	i	h	g	f	e	d	c	b	a

The message *Do you have a secret for me?* becomes *wl blf szev z hvxivg uli nv.* But cipher breakers might guess that single-letter words in the ciphered message

represent /ˌreprɪˈzent/ (v) to be a sign for something
alphabet /ˈælfəbet/ (n) all the letters that are used when writing a language

are either *a* or *I*. They might also guess that two-letter pairs are common words like *or, as, do, of* or *to*. To make the cipher more difficult, you can run the letters together: *wlblfszevzhvxivgulinv*. Or you can break them into groups of four letters each: *wlbl fsze vzhv xivg ulin v*.

Instead of letters, you can use numbers or symbols. You can write *1* for *a, 2* for *b* to make the message: 9 8 1 22 5 1 19 5 3 18 5 20 6 15 18 25 15 21. Your friends will be able to decipher the message as *ihaveasecretforyou*. By adding spaces and a capital letter, they will have the true message: *I have a secret for you.*

Another kind of cipher is shown below. You write the numbers, symbols or letters in **rows** from left to right, with empty squares for spaces:

1	2	3	4	5
i		h	a	v
e		a		s
e	c	r	e	t
	f	o	r	
y	o	u		

Then you write the letters from top to bottom, so the message becomes *iee y cfoharoua er vst*. To make it more difficult, you can agree that your friend will change the order of the **columns** from 1, 2, 3, 4, 5 to 5, 3, 4, 1, 2 so the message becomes *vst harou a er iee y cfo*.

● The Vigenère cipher

Although these ciphers seem hard to understand at first, a patient enemy could break them quite easily. A Frenchman, Blaise de Vigenère, invented the next big step in code-making in the 1500s. Vigenère used rows of alphabets; each row started with a new letter. This part of the cipher was not a secret. The secret part was a code word, like *SMILE*. After you choose your code word, you can start to write your message in cipher. Find the column headed by the first letter of your message and move straight down to the place where the column meets the row that begins with *S* (the first letter of SMILE). That is your first letter. The next letter comes from the row that starts with *M*. Vigenère's cipher looked like the one on the next page.

---

row /rəʊ/ (n) a line of things or people next to each other
column /ˈkɒləm/ (n) a list of words or numbers written below each other down a page

		A	B	C	D	E	F	G	H	**I**	J	K	L	M	N	O	P	Q	R	S	T	U	V	**W**	X	Y	Z
A	•	A	B	C	D	E	F	G	H	I	J	K	L	M	N	O	P	Q	R	S	T	U	V	W	X	Y	Z
B	•	B	C	D	E	F	G	H	I	J	K	L	M	N	O	P	Q	R	S	T	U	V	W	X	Y	Z	A
C	•	C	D	E	F	G	H	I	J	K	L	M	N	O	P	Q	R	S	T	U	V	W	X	Y	Z	A	B
D	•	D	E	F	G	H	I	J	K	L	M	N	O	P	Q	R	S	T	U	V	W	X	Y	Z	A	B	C
E	•	E	F	G	H	I	J	K	L	M	N	O	P	Q	R	S	T	U	V	W	X	Y	Z	A	B	C	D
F	•	F	G	H	I	J	K	L	M	N	O	P	Q	R	S	T	U	V	W	X	Y	Z	A	B	C	D	E
G	•	G	H	I	J	K	L	M	N	O	P	Q	R	S	T	U	V	W	X	Y	Z	A	B	C	D	E	F
H	•	H	I	J	K	L	M	N	O	P	Q	R	S	T	U	V	W	X	Y	Z	A	B	C	D	E	F	G
I	•	I	J	K	L	M	N	O	P	**Q**	R	S	T	U	V	W	X	Y	Z	A	B	C	D	E	F	G	H
J	•	J	K	L	M	N	O	P	Q	R	S	T	U	V	W	X	Y	Z	A	B	C	D	E	F	G	H	I
K	•	K	L	M	N	O	P	Q	R	S	T	U	V	W	X	Y	Z	A	B	C	D	E	F	G	H	I	J
L	•	L	M	N	O	P	Q	R	S	T	U	V	W	X	Y	Z	A	B	C	D	E	F	G	H	I	J	K
M	•	M	N	O	P	Q	R	S	T	U	V	W	X	Y	Z	A	B	C	D	E	F	G	H	**I**	J	K	L
N	•	N	O	P	Q	R	S	T	U	V	W	X	Y	Z	A	B	C	D	E	F	G	H	I	J	K	L	M
O	•	O	P	Q	R	S	T	U	V	W	X	Y	Z	A	B	C	D	E	F	G	H	I	J	K	L	M	N
P	•	P	Q	R	S	T	U	V	W	X	Y	Z	A	B	C	D	E	F	G	H	I	J	K	L	M	N	O
Q	•	Q	R	S	T	U	V	W	X	Y	Z	A	B	C	D	E	F	G	H	I	J	K	L	M	N	O	P
R	•	R	S	T	U	V	W	X	Y	Z	A	B	C	D	E	F	G	H	I	J	K	L	M	N	O	P	Q
S	•	S	T	U	V	W	X	Y	Z	**A**	B	C	D	E	F	G	H	I	J	K	L	M	N	O	P	Q	R
T	•	T	U	V	W	X	Y	Z	A	B	C	D	E	F	G	H	I	J	K	L	M	N	O	P	Q	R	S
U	•	U	V	W	X	Y	Z	A	B	C	D	E	F	G	H	I	J	K	L	M	N	O	P	Q	R	S	T
V	•	V	W	X	Y	Z	A	B	C	D	E	F	G	H	I	J	K	L	M	N	O	P	Q	R	S	T	U
W	•	W	X	Y	Z	A	B	C	D	E	F	G	H	I	J	K	L	M	N	O	P	Q	R	S	T	U	V
X	•	X	Y	Z	A	B	C	D	E	F	G	H	I	J	K	L	M	N	O	P	Q	R	S	T	U	V	W
Y	•	Y	Z	A	B	C	D	E	F	G	H	I	J	K	L	M	N	O	P	Q	R	S	T	U	V	W	X
Z	•	Z	A	B	C	D	E	F	G	H	I	J	K	L	M	N	O	P	Q	R	S	T	U	V	W	X	Y

The message *I will not tell,* using *smile* as the code word, looks like this:

- Codeword: s mile smi lesm
- Sentence: I will not tell
- Cipher text: a iqwp fab eidx

It took a long time to write a message in the Vigenère cipher, but it was very difficult to decipher. It is useful that a letter like *l* in the sentence above is represented by four different letters. That makes it difficult to find the solution unless you know or can guess the code word.

But this was also an important weakness of the Vigenère cipher. People often chose words that were easy to remember. If you knew enough about the person, then you would probably guess that his or her secret code word was the name of a friend, a family member, a hero, a place or even a hobby.

Like all secret codes and ciphers, the Vigenère cipher was only as good as the people who knew it. If one person was forced to share the secret code word, then the cipher was easy to break.

CHAPTER 2

War Secrets

Many of history's secret codes and ciphers – and the ways of breaking them – have probably been lost.

C ompanies keep business secrets. People like to keep personal secrets. But some of the world's most important secrets are about war.

When countries decide to fight each other, it is always important for them to keep their plans secret. During a war, soldiers also need to share their plans in secret. To keep secrets, governments and armies need codes and ciphers that are easy to use but hard to break. But they also need to understand the many ways of breaking enemy codes and ciphers.

● Breaking the Vigenère cipher

Many people thought that the Vigenère cipher was unbreakable. It was used for 300 years before the English scientist Charles Babbage discovered how to break it. But he never told anyone about his secret method – or did he? Some people believe that he told the British government.

From 1854 to 1856, the Ottomans (in the area that is now Turkey), Britain, France and Austria fought in the Crimean War against Russia. The war started after Russia sent part of its army to Turkey. Thousands of soldiers fought around the area of the Black Sea in southern Russia. The Russians used the Vigenère cipher and lost the war. Perhaps their enemies were able to break the cipher and read their messages.

Many of history's secret codes and ciphers – and the ways of breaking them – have probably been lost. After a war, no government wants to share this information; the codes may be needed again. But people did not mind writing about them when both sides knew that they had been broken.

● An early war cipher

One of the first records of the use of a secret cipher in war was in Greece. About 2,400 years ago, soldiers in the Spartan army stretched a long piece of paper around a stick. Then they wrote the letters of a message along the length of the stick. When the paper was taken off, the letters were in an odd order. The letters seemed to make no sense.

Spartan soldiers hid these messages around their waist, under their belts. If they could not escape from an enemy, they would destroy the paper. Even if enemy soldiers found the paper, they needed to stretch the paper around the same size stick to understand the message.

A Spartan war cipher with a message in English

● Caesar's cipher

A little more than 2,000 years ago, the Roman leader Julius Caesar invented another cipher. Caesar needed to send messages to his soldiers but wanted to make sure that no one could read them easily. He **developed** a simple cipher in which letters of the alphabet were moved a few letters forward. For example:

a b c d e f g h i j k l m n o p q r s t u v w x y z
d e f g h i j k l m n o p q r s t u v w x y z a b c

This type of cipher was very easy to break; the enemy simply had to try each of the twenty-five letters after *a* as the starting letter. But Caesar probably did not care for two reasons. First, most of his enemies could not read or write - but they might recognise a few words if a simple cipher was not used. And, second, most of his messages were probably only important for a short time. By the time Caesar's enemies understood a message, it was too late for them to do anything about it.

develop /dɪˈveləp/ (v) to make a new product or idea successful

A more complicated cipher is an arrangement of letters in a different order.

a b c d e f g h i j k l m n o p q r s t u v w x y z
w o g x h p b q r i j y s z c t k d u l v e m f n a

But this cipher still has problems. When you look at a message, you will notice that some letters appear more often than others. In English, *e* is the most common letter. Also, messages need more than just words. What is the difference between these two messages?

Kill the king.

Kill the king?

One message is a command to *kill the king* and the other asks *should someone kill the king?* So, it is useful to add these symbols: ? ! , . : ;

It is also useful to include the numbers zero to nine as part of a cipher. If some words are used often, then they can also have their own code. For example, if an army often uses a word like **submarine**, then it may want to invent a special word or symbol for it.

Often ciphers contain letters that do not mean anything. These can be used in two ways. Messages are often written with no breaks between the letters.

Thesoldiersarenowhere.

But what two meanings could this message have? It makes a difference where you put the spaces between words. If you put them before the first *s*, *a* and *n*, the message says *The soldiers are nowhere.* But if you put them before the first *s*, *a*, *n* and the *h*, the message says something quite different: *The soldiers are now here.* For this reason, you can add extra symbols, numbers or letters to show where the spaces should go.

These extra symbols are also sometimes added to confuse someone trying to read the code. If you and the other person know that the & sign means nothing, you can use it and a few other odd symbols to break up words. You can also use wrong spellings to maake it haardor too deesifer.*

● **Waving flags**

More than 2,000 years ago, Greek and Roman armies used lights and flags to send messages. One message could be sent to many different people. If the **signals** were in code or cipher, an army could send different messages to its soldiers right in front of their enemies. But both lights and flags could only be

* maake it haardor too deesifer: make it harder to decipher

submarine /ˈsʌbməriːn, sʌbməˈriːn/ (n) a ship that can travel under water

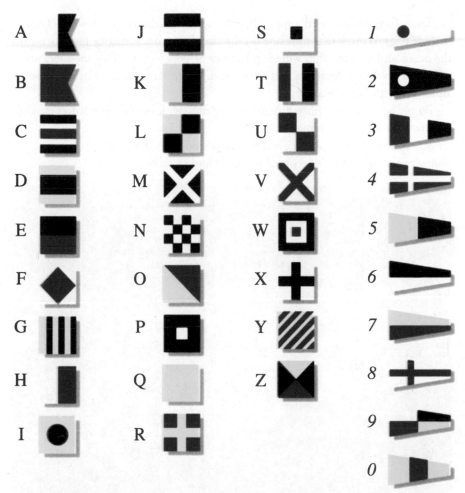

Signal flags

seen over short distances. Around the year 1600, the **telescope** became popular and let people send and receive messages over greater distances.

Before radio, it was difficult to send and receive messages on a ship, especially during wartime. Ships used many kinds of flags to share information or give orders. The most famous flag message was a nine-word code ordered by Horatio Nelson, before he fought at Trafalgar in 1805: 'England expects that every man will do his duty.'

signal /ˈsɪɡnəl/ (n) a sound, action or event that gives information or tells someone to do something
telescope /ˈteləskəʊp/ (n) a piece of equipment like a tube that makes things seem closer or larger

These flags are still used, especially when a ship's radio does not work. They include flags to show that someone on the ship is ill, that someone has fallen into the ocean and that the ship will soon leave or arrive at a port. Flag messages are still often used as decorations and there are different flags for each letter of the alphabet to spell out messages.

People became very quick at sending flag messages, but it was not fast enough. A faster way was to use **semaphore**.

Semaphore flags let people spell messages using the letters of the alphabet. Some letters are also used to signal numbers and mistakes.

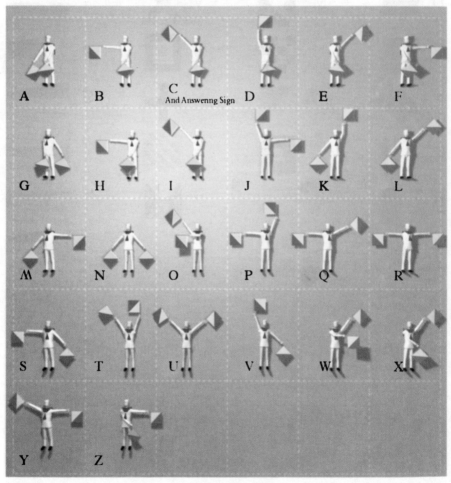

Semaphore flags

semaphore /ˈseməfɔː/ (n) a method of signalling using two handheld flags

The flags are usually square and in two colours. On land, the flags are usually red and white. On the ocean, the flags are usually red and yellow. They are held like the hands of a clock and there are seven positions for each flag.

● The wrong message

Not all secret messages are meant for your friends. Sometimes an army or group of soldiers will send a false message. Often, these false messages help to discover what the enemy knows or is doing.

During World War 2, Americans believed that the Japanese were going to send their ships to attack Midway Island or Alaska in June, 1942. The Americans already knew the Japanese ciphers and the Japanese had communicated about an attack in their secret messages. But the Japanese messages did not say *where* they were going to attack.

To find out, the Americans sent a message using an old code – one they knew that the Japanese had already broken. The message said that Midway Island's water treatment plant was not working.

Soon, the Japanese began sending messages about the need for water on Midway Island. They were worried that there would not be enough water for their army after they made their surprise attack. The Americans listened to these radio messages and knew that the Japanese planned to attack Midway Island. They sent their ships to Midway and destroyed Japan's ships and planes.

2.1 Were you right?

What are the popular uses of secret codes and ciphers? Use the words in the box to complete the sentences.

> war   cipher   flags   prices   secret   stop   alphabets
> text messaging   semaphore   soldiers   clothes

Many codes are not [1] ....; often people *want* you to
understand. Examples are the different symbols for [2] ....,
and foreign languages. Even your [3] .... are a kind of code.
They give people information about you. And we use [4] ....
on mobile phones just to save time. It is the same with [5] ....
on ships which are used to send messages, often by [6] ....
But some codes *are* meant to be secret. Business people use secret ciphers to hide
details about [7] .... Governments use secret codes in
times of [8] .... Caesar used a [9] ....
to send messages to his [10] .... The Vigenère cipher used
rows of [11] .... and was not broken for 300 years.

2.2 What more did you learn?

Decipher these three messages:

2.3 Language in use

Look at these examples of passive forms in the box on the right. Then choose the best passive form of the verb to complete these sentences.

> These flags **are** still **used** ...
> If one person **was forced** to share the secret code, ...

1   The most common codes are in your wallet and they .... *are used* ....
    (use) every day.

2   Not all codes .... (mean) to be secret.

3   Bar codes .... (use) in shops for many years, and still are.

4   By the middle of the nineteenth century, the Vigenère cipher
    .... (use) by the Russians for over 300 years before it was
    dropped.

5   A simple cipher .... (develop) by Caesar to send messages
    to his soldiers.

6   Messages .... (can/decipher) in Sparta by tying the paper
    around a stick.

What's next?

2.4

Look at the pictures. What do you think?

1   Who are the two women?
    ....
    ....

2   What jobs did these women have?
    ....

3   When were these pictures painted?
    ....

4   What problems did the women have
    with each other?
    ....
    ....

5   Why did they use secret codes?
    ....
    ....
    ....

CHAPTER 3

A Queen's Mistake

Instead of helping Mary, Elizabeth sent her to a country house.
Mary was forced to stay there. She was Elizabeth's prisoner.

The sad story of Mary, Queen of Scots shows that it is not always an advantage in life to be royal – or to be skilled in the use of codes.

Mary's father was King James V of Scotland. His wife was French and Mary was born in 1542. Mary's father died when she was just six days old, and when she was a year old she became Queen of the Scots. At five years old, she was sent to France. It was not safe for her in Scotland; England's King Henry VIII wanted to take Scotland, and he began to attack the country.

At the age of fifteen, Mary married Francis, son of the King of France, but he died two years later and she returned to Scotland. Her next marriage was to her Scottish cousin, Henry Stewart, and they had one child, a son. But Stewart made many enemies. These enemies tried to kill him once and failed; the second time, they were successful. Most people thought that one of Stewart's killers was Lord Bothwell.

● **Two queens**

A few months later, Mary married Lord Bothwell. But other lords were angered by his new position and Mary ran away to England to ask for help from her cousin, Elizabeth I. Elizabeth was worried, though, about Mary's Catholic religion. England's kings and queens had also followed the Catholic religion until Elizabeth's father, Henry VIII, had made England a Protestant country. So many English Catholics wanted Mary to be queen of England, not Elizabeth. Instead of helping Mary, Elizabeth sent her to a country house. Mary was forced to stay there. She was Elizabeth's prisoner.

Mary was not punished in any way and even had servants to help her, but she could not travel or have visitors without Elizabeth's permission. Years passed and Mary began to understand that she would die as a prisoner.

Still, she had some hope. The Catholic king of Spain, Philip II, was ready to attack England after Elizabeth died. French armies also wanted to attack England but were afraid of Elizabeth. And there were many people in England who did not want Elizabeth to be their queen. Both Mary and Elizabeth heard news about these unhappy people from their own spies. The kings and queens of England had had spies since 1324, when King Edward II ordered all letters to or from England to be opened and read.

Queen Elizabeth I   *Mary, Queen of Scots*

● A royal cipher

Mary had a special way to get news from her friends and supporters. Every few days, Gilbert Gifford delivered lemonade to the house where Mary stayed. He left full lemonade containers and picked up the empty ones. But they were not completely empty. Both the full containers and the empty ones often had secret notes hidden in them. Mary's servants put one message inside a container and took another out.

Gifford's job was to deliver the messages between Mary and her spy, Anthony Babington. Babington had many contacts among important people who wanted to kill Elizabeth. But he and Mary both knew they had to be careful. If anyone found the messages, then Babington would certainly be killed. Even Mary might be killed. Instead of writing in plain English, Mary used her own personal secret cipher.

Mary's cipher used numbers and symbols for twenty-three letters of the alphabet – there were no symbols for *j*, *v* or *w*. There were also symbols that meant nothing. These could be used between words as spaces or just to confuse anyone reading the message. Mary also had twenty-four other symbols that were used as codes for her name and for common words, and one symbol to show double letters.

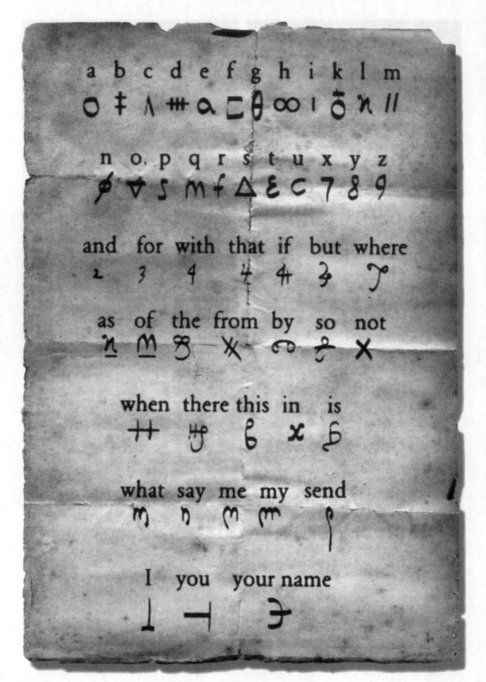

The cipher of Mary, Queen of Scots

Mary thought that no one would find her secret messages, but she was wrong. She also thought that if anyone found the messages, then they would not be able to read her secret cipher, but she was wrong again. Gilbert Gifford was really working for Elizabeth's secretary, Sir Francis Walsingham.

Walsingham wanted to get rid of Mary but knew that Elizabeth was afraid of killing a Catholic queen. She thought it would anger other Catholic kings and queens and perhaps start a war with the rest of Europe. She was also afraid that Elizabeth's own people would not like it and would fight against her. Walsingham needed clear information to show that Mary wanted to kill Elizabeth and he found it in the secret letters.

● The final message

When Gifford received a letter from Mary, he gave it to Walsingham before he gave it to Babington. Walsingham gave it to Thomas Phelippes, a language specialist. Phelippes was good at breaking secret ciphers. He copied the message and he and his team started working on it. Each letter was quickly returned to Gifford so he could give it to Babington. It was important that Mary and Babington should not notice an unusual delay.

Phelippes studied the ciphered messages using a method developed by an Arab code breaker named Abu Yusuf al-Kindi. When al-Kindi looked at different languages, he discovered that some letters were used much more than others. In English, the order of the most common letters is: *e, t, a, o, i, n, s, h, r, d, l, u.* The letter *e* usually appears about thirteen times in one hundred letters. The least common letter, *z*, only appears once.

Phelippes quickly deciphered the message by finding some letters and guessing at others. Soon, Walsingham could read everything that Mary and Babington wrote. Babington explained his plans to kill Queen Elizabeth as well as Walsingham and others. Mary wrote back and said she understood. This was the message Walsingham was waiting for. But Babington wrote about six other men who would help him. Walsingham wanted to know their names too.

Walsingham asked Phelippes to add a few sentences to the letter before Gifford gave it to Babington. Phelippes used Mary's code and copied her handwriting. In the new message, Phelippes asked Babington for the names of the other six men.

Perhaps Babington knew that something was wrong. He tried to leave England for Spain but was taken prisoner. He and twelve other men were hanged. The next year, Mary was taken to a special court. At first, she was calm and said she knew nothing about the plans to kill Elizabeth or to invite the

Spanish king to attack England. But then the court showed Mary her own letters and she could not deny it. At the age of forty-four, Mary had her head cut off.

● A secret diary

Many other people have used personal ciphers, for different reasons. One famous cipher was used by Samuel Pepys. His cousin got him a job in the government in London. Pepys was intelligent and a hard worker and he was soon given better and better jobs. In time, he became a friend of the king of England, Charles II. Pepys was a witness to many exciting events in the history of England, like the Great Fire of London. During this fire, much of the city burned down.

In 1659, Pepys was twenty-seven years old and he decided to start writing a diary. He wrote his diary in a cipher so others could not read it – especially his wife! He used different symbols and he also mixed words from English, French and Portuguese as a kind of a code. Pepys wrote for himself and not for a newspaper or because he wanted to sell his diary in bookshops. So he did not try to make things sound better or worse than they really were. Today, Pepys's diaries give us a clear picture of an important time in English history.

● Remembering ciphers

Pepys's cipher was common when he lived, but after he died in 1703 his diaries were not read for more than a hundred years. By then, no one remembered the cipher. Finally, in 1819, a man named Thomas Shelton spent three years deciphering the diaries. Sadly, he did not know that the cipher key was in another book on a bookshelf above the diaries!

A big problem with ciphers is teaching people how to understand and remember them. Until 1915, the Russian army used an old cipher that was easy to break because poorly trained Russian soldiers could not remember newer ciphers. The Chinese general Sun Tzu had faced the same problem 2,500 years earlier. He used the first forty words of a poem. After soldiers learned the poem, it was easy to teach them that each word in the poem was a code word for something else.

● Mistakes

The stories of Mary, Queen of Scots, Samuel Pepys and the Russians show how one cannot always be confident about secret codes and ciphers. Mary believed that no one would ever discover the secret of her royal cipher. She knew enough to use a secret cipher, but not enough to understand that it could be broken. That mistake cost her life.

Mary's cipher did not protect her because she did not know the people who worked with her well enough. It was easy for one so-called friend to work with her enemies.

Samuel Pepys had the opposite problem. He wrote in cipher only to stop his wife from reading about his private life. When he left directions to give his books to Cambridge University, he wanted someone to read his diaries. But the diaries were almost lost and forgotten.

It is hard to understand the Russian Army's use of an old cipher that they knew their enemies could decipher. Why did they not develop a new cipher or code? No one will ever know.

CHAPTER 4

Unsolved Codes and Ciphers

The letter explained that the box contained secret information about a fortune in gold, silver and jewels.

In 1885, a small but unusual book was printed in the United States. It was called *The Beale Papers*. It tells a very strange story about a mysterious lost fortune.

The mystery began in 1820 with a man called Robert Morriss. Morriss owned a hotel in Lynchburg, Virginia, in the United States. One day, he had a few new visitors to his hotel, Thomas Jefferson Beale and his friends. Beale was intelligent and kind. He stayed for about ten days and became friends with Morriss. Morriss said later that Beale was a handsome man but that his face was very dark, like the face of a man who had spent a lot of time in the sun.

Beale left but he returned after two years and asked Morriss to keep something for him. It was a small locked metal box and Beale told his friend that there were important papers inside. A little later, Beale sent Morriss a letter.

The letter explained that the box contained secret information about a fortune in gold, silver and jewels. Beale promised to send the key for the box and information for decoding the messages inside it. The letter also said that Morriss should open the box in ten years if Beale did not return.

Beale did not return. Nothing was ever heard from him again. He did not send the key and he did not explain the secrets. Morriss guessed that Native Americans* had killed Beale. But he forgot about the box and did not open it until 1845.

The box contained a few letters and other papers, including three pages of numbers. Morriss did not understand the pages of numbers, but one of the letters was quite exciting.

● An explanation

The letter said that in 1818 Beale and about thirty other men had travelled in the American Southwest. Somewhere around Santa Fe, New Mexico, they had found gold and silver – lots of it! They **traded** some of the heavy silver for lighter jewels and took everything to the eastern United States. They then **buried** their fortune in a secret place in the ground where no one would find it.

The letter also explained the three pages of numbers. The first page, it said, described where the secret fortune was buried. The second page explained what

---

* Native Americans: the first people to live in North America

trade /treɪd/ (v) to buy or sell large quantities of things
bury /'beri/ (v) to put a dead body under ground

was included in the fortune. The third page gave the names of the people who should share the gold, silver and jewels. These were the relatives of the men who found the fortune.

● Giving away secrets

Morriss could not work out the strange numbers on the secret pages. For many years he tried to understand them, but he did not know where to start. In 1862, he gave the box and its papers to another man, J B Ward, to look at.

Ward found a **clue** to the second of the three pages. He decided that there were too many numbers for them to be ciphers for letters. Instead, he guessed that each number represented a word in a book. The question was: which book?

Ward decided that it must be a popular or famous book or document that anyone could find. Also it must be one that existed when Beale wrote his pages of numbers. He started looking at different books and documents to see if one had words that matched the numbers in a meaningful way. Finally, he found an American government document that matched the second page of numbers.

Ward compared the numbers and words and finally understood one of the three parts of the secret. This second page explained that the fortune was in Bedford, Virginia. It included 460 kilograms of gold, and 1,729 kilograms of silver. There were also many jewels.

The letter also explained that the gold, silver and jewels were 'packed in iron pots with iron covers'. All the pots were buried in a hole in the ground, about two metres deep, and covered with stones. The message said that the exact place was given in the first page of numbers.

But the government document did not give clues to the first or the third pages of numbers. Ward tried to find answers for the next twenty-three years, but he failed. In 1885, he explained everything in his book.

People became very excited about the mystery of *The Beale Papers*. Many did not wait to solve the mystery of the first page. They started to dig all around Bedford. The townspeople dug up their own gardens and farms.

But the fortune has never been found. Even today, people still look for it. In today's money, the value of the gold, silver and jewels is about £10,000,000.

● A big joke?

Cipher breakers continue to look for solutions to the first and third pages in books as well as in other places. For example, old stories from Native Americans in the west of the United States talked about people taking their gold to the east

---

clue /kluː/ (n) something, or a piece of information, that helps to solve a crime or other problem

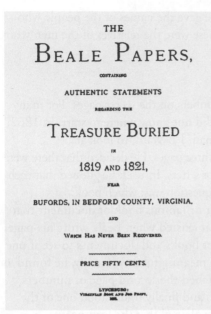

The cover of The Beale Papers, *printed by Ward*

of the country. Were these old stories about Beale? Perhaps the other pages are not the same kind of book code.

But other people think the Beale story is not true – that *The Beale Papers* is just a joke. They have looked for information about Morriss, Beale and Ward. Morriss was probably a real person, but little information can be found about Beale or Ward. Some people say it is not likely that gold was found where the letter says it was. And why did Beale write letters in three different ciphers? Why not just use one? There are a lot of questions.

Language specialists say that Beale uses words in his letter that were not popular in 1822. Perhaps someone else – not Beale – wrote the letters much later. But why would anyone go to so much trouble?

One reason might be money – but not for the fortune-hunters. Ward's book was very popular and made him a lot of money. Perhaps he simply made up the story. At the end of the *The Beale Papers*, Ward gives some good advice. He warns readers not to waste too much time looking for clues.

● The Voynich Manuscript

Twenty-seven years after Ward's Beale Papers book came out, an American book collector, Wilfred Voynich, visited an old house outside Rome, in Italy. He found an old manuscript that was handwritten sometime around the 15th century.

The pages of the book are about the size of this book's pages, but the Voynich Manuscript is much thicker and much more difficult to understand. It is completely in cipher. No one has been able to understand it.

Pages from the Voynich Manuscript

manuscript /ˈmænjʊskrɪpt/ (n) an old book written by hand before printing was invented

The Voynich Manuscript is also filled with very unusual pictures. Many of them look like scientific drawings of plants and views from telescopes. But there are also many small, odd pictures of women in baths. The baths are connected like the branches of plants. One solution may be to study as many old European languages as possible and search for a cipher that fits.

● A musical cipher?

The British musician Edward Elgar liked **puzzles** and secret codes. He even put them into some of his music. On 14 July 1897, Elgar sent a letter to Miss

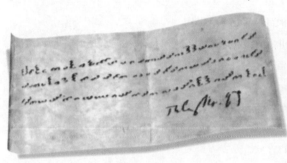

Elgar's cipher

Dora Penny, the daughter of a friend of Elgar's wife. The letter included a cipher.

Penny was not able to decipher the message and Elgar never gave her the answer. To guess the meaning, people have looked at what Elgar and Penny both knew about and liked: walking in the countryside, football, horse racing and music. But Penny was not a very good musician and Elgar would not send her a musical message that was too difficult to decipher. Elgar died in 1934 and Penny died in 1964.

● The Zodiac Cipher

In the 1960s and 1970s, the Zodiac Killer murdered at least five people in California. After he killed them, he wrote letters to police departments and newspapers. In his letters, he talked about how he killed the people. He also included messages in cipher.

Each cipher was handwritten on paper. Most of the symbols are letters, but some are squares, circles and other shapes. Some are filled in and others have **dots** in them. Some of the cipher text has been broken. We now know that the killer used seven different symbols for the letter *E* and did not have any symbols for some other letters.

The killer explained that one of the codes gave his real name, but no one has been able to discover it. There are many unsolved ciphers. Perhaps you will solve them one day.

puzzle /'pʌzəl/ (n) something that is difficult to understand or explain
dot /dɒt/ (n) a small round mark or spot

3.1 Were you right?

Check your answers to Activity 2.4. Then number these events in the correct order.

☐ Elizabeth finds and deciphers the secret messages.
☐ Elizabeth has Mary's head cut off.
☐ Elizabeth makes Mary her prisoner.
☐ Mary escapes to England.
☐ Mary is born in Scotland.
☐ Mary marries Henry Stewart. He is later killed.
☐ Mary marries Lord Bothwell, possibly the killer of Henry Stewart.
☐ Mary marries the son of the King of France.
☐ Mary sends secret messages.
☐ The son of the King of France dies.

What more did you learn?

3.2 Are these sentences true (T) or false (F)?

1 Robert Morriss discovered the Beale fortune. **T F**

2 Pages of numbers may tell everything about the Beale fortune. **T F**

3 A government document was the key to one of the pages. **T F**

4 The Voynich Manuscript is written in an English cipher. **T F**

5 Knowledge of Elgar and Penny's shared interests might help solve Elgar's cipher. **T F**

6 The Zodiac Killer wrote ciphered messages about his murders. **T F**

7 The Zodiac Killer's cipher included nine symbols for the letter E. **T F**

3.3 Language in use

Look at the sentence in the box. Then use *by* + V-*ing* in these sentences.

> He deciphered the message **by finding** some letters and **guessing** others.

1 They kept Mary safe ....*by sending*.........(send) her to France when she was five years old.

2 Mary sent messages ....(put) them in empty containers.

3 Pepys kept his diary secret .... (write) it in a cipher.

4 .... (read) Pepys' diaries we have a better understanding of life at that time.

5 Beale discovered that the secret fortune was very large .... (decipher) a page of numbers.

6 The Zodiac Killer angered the police .... (send) them messages in code.

3.4 What's next?

Look closely. What do you see in each picture? Write your answers.

....
....

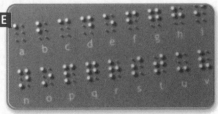

....
....

CHAPTER 5

Hidden Writing

Britain's spy department quickly contacted Dawes. He was not a German spy
and he did not have special information – but his students did!

Secret codes and ciphers are not the only ways to hide secrets. Often, people do not use secret codes at all. Instead, they hide the messages that they want to send. For example, a Greek king wrote a message to another king on the shaved head of a **slave**. The slave's hair grew back and he travelled to see the second king. The second king shaved his head and read the message. This was an unusual way to send a message and it was not very fast.

● Secret inks

There are many other interesting ways to hide secret messages. For example, you can use inks that cannot be seen. Most paper money now uses these kinds of inks. When you hold paper money up to a special light, you can read extra information.

You can use another kind of secret ink at home. Simply write your message in orange juice or milk and let it dry. The writing should then disappear and you can send your secret message to your friends. When your friends receive the message, they can warm it gently over a toaster. The heat will make the hidden writing appear again. But be careful not to burn the paper!

If an enemy saw a plain piece of paper in the mail, he would wonder what it was all about. So it is better to write a false letter with unimportant information in it. Make the lines of your sentences a little wider and write your true message between them.

● Cheap messages

Another way to send a hidden message is to write an ordinary message but mark certain letters. Many years ago, it was inexpensive to send newspapers in England but expensive to send letters. People found an interesting way to save money. They used a needle to make small holes under different letters. The message could be anywhere in the newspaper. You only needed a story with all the letters for your message in the right order. For example,

> Charlbury's most beautiful garden, at this time of year, is an old one: wild Cornbury Park.

slave /sleɪv/ (n) someone who is owned by another person and must work for them without payment; *slavery* is the use of *slaves* or the condition of being a *slave*

When the underlined letters are taken out, the message becomes *meetmeinlondon*. With spaces and capital letters added, the message becomes clear: *Meet me in London.* Can you read the message in the lines below?

The me<u>ss</u>age <u>c</u>ould be much mo<u>re</u> difficul<u>t</u> if you also u<u>s</u>ed <u>a</u> ciphe<u>r</u>. It would also h<u>e</u>lp if you m<u>a</u>de ho<u>l</u>es under <u>l</u>etters on other p<u>a</u>ges, so an enemy would not know which page to look at.

A simil<u>ar</u> way to hide a message is t<u>o</u> cut holes in two pieces of plain paper. Yo<u>u</u> give o<u>n</u>e of the pieces to your frien<u>d</u> and keep the other piece. Yo<u>u</u> then put a piece of writing paper under the piece with the hole<u>s</u> and write your message. When you take away the top piece of paper, the one underneath has your message. To hide it, you write in other words between the words of your message.

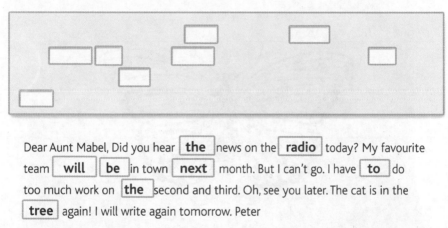

Dear Aunt Mabel, Did you hear **the** news on the **radio** today? My favourite team **will** **be** in town **next** month. But I can't go. I have **to** do too much work on **the** second and third. Oh, see you later. The cat is in the **tree** again! I will write again tomorrow. Peter

● A dangerous word puzzle

In 1945, a British newspaper printed a word puzzle by a schoolteacher called Leonard Dawe. The answers to the puzzle included five unusual words: the names of an American state, an American city, an unusual tree and the Roman god of the sea, and a word for a leader. It was near the end of World War 2 and the British and Americans were worried. These five words were all important code words used by their armies in planning attacks against the German army in France.

Britain's spy department quickly contacted Dawes. He was not a German spy and he did not have special information – but his students did! They had suggested the words and helped Dawes write the puzzle. Where did they learn the words? Dawes's students liked to play around a British army camp and had often heard soldiers use the code words. The students did not know what the words meant, but thought they sounded important. They had not told Dawes where they heard the words.

● Coded pictures

Not all messages can be written in code. Sometimes spies need to send pictures. In 1892, soldiers at an important German army building in Dalmatia, on the Mediterranean Sea, enjoyed laughing at Robert Baden-Powell. He ran all around the fields outside the building and explained his insect drawings to anyone who was interested.

But his drawings were more important. They were really drawings of the building, showing the position of each gate and big gun. They were just drawn to look like insects. At other times, Baden-Powell hid a drawing of another building by making it look like an old church window.

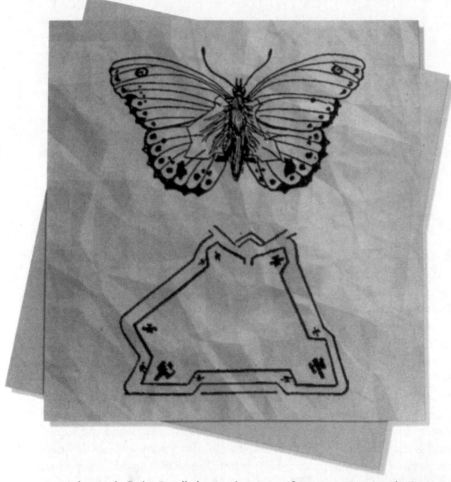

A drawing by Baden-Powell, showing the position of army guns on an insect's wings

Baden-Powell was a spy for many years in India, Africa and Europe. In 1915, he wrote a book about his life, *My Adventures as a Spy.* He described many ways of hiding messages. In Africa, he wrote his messages on small pieces of paper and made them into balls. These were hidden in holes in walking sticks or covered in small, thin sheets of metal and worn around a messenger's neck. If an enemy stopped you, you could drop the balls and they looked like small stones. Later, you could return and pick them up.

Another method was to write the two arms of semaphore symbols and connect several symbols in a line. These lines could be fitted onto the side of a drawing.

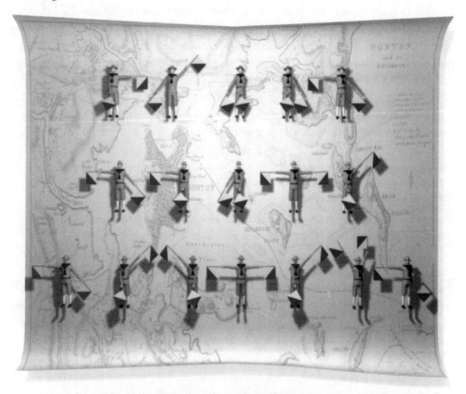

A semaphore message: 'Flags share secrets'

Because he was good at spying, Baden-Powell was also good at catching other spies. In his book, he explains how people used lights and chimney smoke to send signals. Sometimes, they carried lights into fields to send signals. If anyone asked, they would pretend to look for a lost animal. When Baden-Powell died, a circle with a dot was put on the stone where he was buried. It is code for 'gone home'.

● Strange places

Secrets have been hidden in many different places, even in food! In the year 1280, Kublai Khan and the Mongols became the rulers of China. The Chinese became their slaves. In 1368, the Chinese decided to fight back. To share their plans, they asked all their bakers to hide messages in special cakes served during the August Moon celebrations. Only the Chinese ate these mooncakes – not the Mongols. Inside each mooncake was a piece of paper with the message, 'Kill all the Mongols!' The Chinese people started a war and won. They became the rulers of the country again.

Many spies carried secrets in hidden places. When the enemy searched them, their secrets would not be noticed. During World War 2, doctors visited prisoners and brought them new clothes. They took the old clothes with them. But the prisoners often wrote secret messages in very small letters on parts of their old clothes. The doctors found these and gave them to the prisoners' governments and families.

The backs of shirt and coat buttons were another popular place to hide secret messages. If an enemy was near, you would tear off the secret button and destroy it or throw it away. Often, spies used ordinary things like pencils and coins with hollow spaces to hide messages.

Photographs are more difficult to hide. But after very small cameras were invented, their pictures could be made into small dots. These dots were hidden in unlikely places. One favourite place was behind a stamp on a letter. Other photographic dots were sometimes hidden somewhere on a spy's body.

Now a photograph or page of text can be hidden inside another photograph and then sent by computer. Only a computer with the right code can read the information. At one business, a boss wondered about one of his employees. The employee sent **email** messages with pictures to his 'grandmother' every day. It was strange that she never wrote back. Finally, the boss found out that the employee was hiding company information in the photographs and sending it to another business.

Computers have made it much easier to hide secrets, but some secrets are hidden where everyone can see them. One spy used code words in a car advertisement to share information about meetings. The message could only be recognised by someone who knew the code. Another spy used coloured pins on a telephone post to give different messages. But while people hide messages, other people will always look for ways to discover them.

email /'iːmeɪl/ (n) electronic mail; a way of sending messages by computer

CHAPTER 6

Secret Symbols

After his African American helper was beaten by a Ku Klux Klan gang,
Kennedy decided to try to destroy the organisation.

What does it mean when you get a letter with the stamp upside down? It may just mean that the sender was in a hurry. But in some countries, like China, it is a sign that there is a secret letter inside.

We are surrounded by secret symbols. Many people never notice most of them. When you get in a lift, you will see a few rows of **raised** dots next to the buttons. You may know that they are for the blind, but what do they mean?

● Writing for the blind

The dots are a way of writing called Braille. It is named after Louis Braille, the man who invented it. Braille was born in a small town near Paris in 1809. His father made shoes for a living. When Braille was four years old, he went into his father's shop and tried to make some shoes. He took a pointed metal tool and made holes in pieces of leather.

Braille had an accident and the tool went into his right eye. Soon after that, he lost sight in the eye. This was bad news, but it got worse. Braille slowly lost sight in his left eye. He was now blind.

For two years, Braille still went to the local school, but he was not learning anything and could not read or write. Braille finally went to a special school for blind boys in Paris. The school was like a prison and the boys were badly beaten for the smallest mistakes. They learned simple jobs that they could do without using their eyes.

The students did not learn how to write, but the school did try to teach them how to read. There were few books for the blind and they all used raised letters on the page. But it was difficult to read them because the letters all felt too similar.

In 1821, Braille met a soldier called Charles Barbier. Barbier had invented a way for soldiers to communicate at night without speaking or using lights. Barbier used twelve raised dots on paper for soldiers to feel. But the cipher was too difficult for soldiers to learn or remember. Braille thought he could make it simpler to help blind people to read. He used different arrangements of six dots for writing letters and numbers and even invented dot ciphers for mathematics and music.

raise /reɪz/ (v) to move or lift something into a higher position

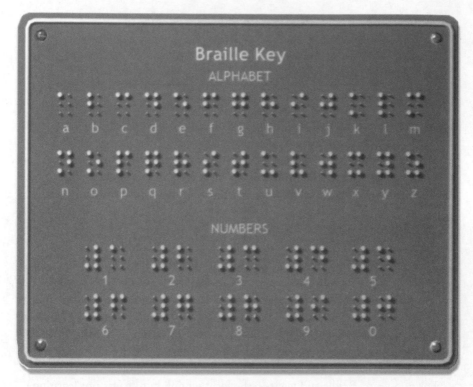

Braille symbols

Braille's alphabet for the blind was not an immediate success. Braille became a teacher at his old school, but another teacher refused to allow his students to learn it. But the students liked the new and easy way to read. They began learning it in secret. Blind people everywhere liked to write messages in their own Braille letters.

Braille writing is now found around the world, on everything from buildings to paper money.

● Hobo signs

Hobos are not so common now, but there used to be a lot of them in North America. They were mostly men, who travelled from place to place to find work. Often, the cheapest way to travel was to jump on a train. But it was against the law and it was dangerous. The train companies did not want to give free rides to hobos. They hired gangs of strong men to get rid of them. Sometimes, the gangs killed the hobos. Sometimes the hobos fell under train wheels as they tried to escape, or they froze in winter.

When hobos went to a new place, they left signs around the town to share information with other hobos. These signs were usually small drawings near the door or gate of a house or business. Most people did not notice them. If they did, they might think that the signs were accidental marks or simply children's drawings.

In this way, the hobos shared information about food, work and dangers.

Hobo symbols

The underground railway

From 1861 to 1865, armies from the North and South of the United States fought each other. The war was mostly about African American slaves. Many people in the South wanted to keep them as cheap workers, but many people in the North wanted the slaves to go free. During this time, slaves escaped from the South and travelled to the North on the 'Underground Railroad'.

hobo /ˈhəʊbəʊ/ (n) someone who travels around and has no home or job

The Underground Railroad was not underground and it was not a railway. It was a group of people who helped slaves escape. It was dangerous to escape and dangerous to help slaves. These helpers had many secret ways to tell slaves where there was a safe house for them to rest. One way was to hang colourful blankets on their washing lines.

These colourful blankets had interesting **pattern**s. Most people thought that they were just pretty. But slaves knew what the patterns meant. A pattern of flying birds showed the best direction to take for an escape to Canada, the first country in the world to make slavery illegal.

Blanket symbols

Go to Canada

When the Underground Railroad was ready for more slaves to escape, the helpers put out blankets with pictures of wheels and tools on them. The wheels meant that it was time to go; the tools meant that the slaves should bring tools to help them. Some tools could help them find new work. Other tools could be used for protection. There were many signs for danger. For example, one pattern warned slaves to change direction often.

Time to go

Bring tools

Change direction often

● **Superman and the Ku Klux Clan**

After the Southern United States lost the war against the North, many people were unhappy that slaves were free. Six white men from the American South decided to start an organisation called the Ku Klux Klan, or KKK. At first, they just met, talked and played games. But soon, the group also began to terrorise and kill freed slaves.

The KKK became very powerful. It did not cost very much to join, but a lot of people, mostly men, did join. They paid a small amount of money that went to the leaders of the KKK. These leaders often used the money for illegal activities. By 1920, 4,000,000 white Americans belonged to the KKK.

Stetson Kennedy was born in 1916. He was an American writer who often wrote about African Americans and he hated the KKK. After his African

pattern /ˈpætən/ (n) shapes that are arranged in a regular way

American helper was beaten by a KKK gang, Kennedy decided to try to destroy the organisation. He started by writing about it but few people were interested. Most thought that nothing could be done to stop the KKK.

In the 1950s, Kennedy decided that he should work against the KKK from the inside of the organisation. He joined under a false name, pretended to be a good member of the group (without hurting anyone) and learned all about the KKK. He gave secret information to the police, politicians and newspapers, and he wrote more about the organisation, but little was done about it.

Then Kennedy had an idea. Would he be more successful if he could make everyone laugh at the KKK? He contacted the makers of *Superman*, a radio show for children. Were they interested in a new enemy for Superman to fight? They were, and Kennedy gave them all the Klan's secret code words. The writers of the radio show and children liked the new story. Soon KKK members' own children were playing Superman and KKK – and the KKK always lost!

When the leaders of the KKK heard their code words on the radio, they quickly changed them. But because Kennedy was a member, he learned the new code words and quickly gave them to the writers of the radio show. The embarrassment hurt the KKK and they soon lost most of their members. No one wanted to belong to a secret group that was not so secret.

Kennedy wrote a book about his fight against the KKK. He sold 400,000 copies. Suddenly, many people learned the facts about the KKK and were not afraid of it anymore. More importantly, it became embarrassing to be a member. This made even more KKK members leave.

4.1 **Were you right?**

Circle the best answer.

1 Hobos used signs to ... .

a help them meet police **b** find the closest train **c** share information

2 Baden Powell was ... .

a a Braille specialist **b** a spy in Australia **c** skilled at hiding secrets

3 Stetson Kennedy helped destroy the KKK ... .

a by making fun of it **b** with secret radios **c** with other slaves

4 Slaves used blankets to ... .

a keep animals warm **b** escape safely **c** catch birds

5 Photographs are sometimes hidden ... .

a in large cameras **b** in other photographs **c** on top of stamps

6 People cut holes in newspapers to ... .

a warn spies **b** destroy unpleasant stories **c** save money

4.2 **What more did you learn?**

Match the people to the things they are known for.

1 ☐ Chinese bakers

2 ☐ Doctors visiting prisoners

3 ☐ Louis Braille

4 ☐ Robert Baden-Powell

5 ☐ Stetson Kennedy

4.3 Language in use

Number the sentences in the correct order. What clues do you use to help you make your choices?

[ ] But be careful not to burn the paper!

[ ] Most paper money now uses these kinds of inks.

[ ] For example, you can use inks that cannot be seen.

[ ] Simply write your message in orange juice or milk and let it dry.

[ ] The heat will make the hidden writing appear again.

[ ] The writing should then disappear and you can send your secret message to your friends.

[1] There are many other interesting ways to hide secret messages.

[ ] When you hold paper money up to a special light, you can read extra information.

[ ] When your friends receive the message, they can warm it gently over a toaster.

[ ] You can use another kind of secret ink at home.

4.4 What's next?

Codes often appear in stories - especially detective stories. Work with other students. Can you think of any stories (books or films, for example) that contain a code? Make notes here.

Notes

CHAPTER 7

Puzzles in Fiction

At first, Holmes thinks the message is in code. But then he sees the meaning.
Every third word is the real message.

The French writer Victor Hugo wrote a book that was **translated** into
English and sold in Britain. He wanted to know how well the book was
selling, so he sent this message to his British bookseller:

?

The bookseller wrote back to tell him that the book was selling very well. His
message was:

!

Many writers also like to use puzzles and secrets in their books.

● Sherlock Holmes

Arthur Conan Doyle's Sherlock Holmes detective stories are full of secret codes
and symbols. In 'The Adventure of the Red Circle', Sherlock Holmes solves a
case by watching a man walk in front of a window with a light. The man shows
the light once, then several more times, before stopping and starting again.
Holmes understands that the man's light is communicating one letter after
another. One light means *a*, two lights mean *b*, three lights mean *c* ...

Even after Holmes has understood this, the letters do not seem to make sense.
Is there a secret cipher or are they code words? Then he realises that the messages
are not in English. They are in Italian. Finally, after a warning is repeated three
times, the message is changed to the word *Danger*. When the message suddenly
stops, Holmes rushes to see what happened. He finds that the man with the light
has been murdered. Holmes uses the light at the window cipher to help solve the
crime.

Lights at a window are also used in another Sherlock Holmes story, *The
Hound of the Baskervilles*. But these lights are used as a simple code to warn a
criminal. In stories by other writers, people often use mirrors to send messages
and warnings.

In Conan Doyle's 'The Five Orange Pips', a man receives a letter with five
orange seeds in it. His nephew, John, does not understand it and watches his
uncle burn a box full of papers. John's uncle soon dies in a mysterious way. Later,
John's father receives a similar letter, also with five orange seeds in it. This letter

translate /trænsˈleɪt, trænz-/ (v) to change speech or writing from one language to another

asks him to put the box and its letters outside. He cannot, because they are already burnt. He soon dies as well. Sherlock Holmes understands that the five orange seeds are a code for 'you will be killed'. He promises to help John, but that night John is also murdered.

'The Musgrave Ritual' contains an unusual puzzle that the detective must solve. Holmes has a friend called Reginald Musgrave. Musgrave has a strange document that has been in his family for a few hundred years. It begins like this:

> *Whose was it?*
>
> *His who is gone.*
>
> *Who shall have it?*
>
> *He who will come.*
>
> *Where was the sun?*

The document then talks about *trees* and *steps* and *directions*. But no one in the Musgrave family has ever understood it. Two people disappear while they are working for Musgrave and Holmes tries to find out what happened. In fact, the document has several map clues to find something that was hidden long ago. It is finally found but looks unimportant: a bag of old metal and stones. But Holmes cleans them and explains that they are the royal jewels of the first kings of England.

In 'The Gloria Scott', Holmes goes to visit his old friend, Victor Trevor. One night, Trevor's father receives a letter. It is a very simple message of just two sentences about hunting birds, but Trevor's father is deeply shocked and he soon dies.

Trevor shows Holmes the letter, but it does not make sense. At first, Holmes thinks the message is in code. But then he sees the meaning. Every third word is the real message. Trevor's father has an enemy who has talked to the police about the father's secret criminal past.

Sherlock Holmes's most famous cipher case is 'The Adventure of the Jumping Men'. In this story, a man comes to Holmes with a copy of a drawing that he has seen around the outside of his house. It is a row of stick figures that appear to be jumping. These jumping men mean nothing to the man, but they upset his wife. She seems to know their secret, but she will not tell him.

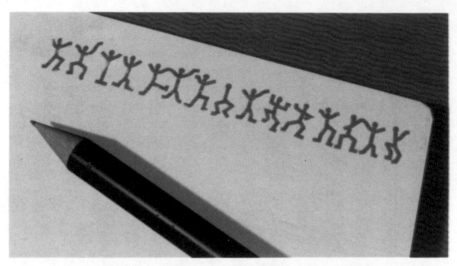

The jumping *men*

Holmes looks at the message and begins to guess what each jumping man might mean. It is a cipher of symbols. Each jumping man is a symbol for a different letter. Soon, Holmes discovers the meaning of the messages. But he is too late. The man is dead and the police think that his wife has killed him. Holmes finds a way to catch the real killer. He uses the jumping Men cipher to send a message to the local hotel. The killer quickly comes there and is caught by the police. Holmes's message is the one above. It means, 'Come here at once.'

The murderer is surprised that anyone can understand his code. Holmes explains that one man's invention can always be understood by another man.

● Edgar Allen Poe

Like Arthur Conan Doyle, Edgar Allen Poe was a writer who was interested in ciphers. He wrote newspaper stories about them and invited readers to send him secret messages in their own ciphers. People were surprised that Poe could read their secret messages. But Poe himself only used very simple ciphers, where one letter or symbol was used for another letter. Later, though, he wrote about how to solve ciphers and his notes were used to break German ciphers during World War 1.

Poe also used a secret cipher in his short story 'The Gold Bug'. In the story, an insect collector draws a picture of an insect he has found. The drawing is on a piece of paper he has also found. But on the other side of the paper is something else: an old clue to something that was buried. After finding a page with secret hidden writing on it and breaking a cipher, the insect collector finds a fortune in gold.

Poe was a writer. Conan Doyle, who wrote the Sherlock Holmes stories, was a doctor, not a detective; he started writing detective stories because not enough sick people came to see him and he needed another way to make money. But the famous British writer Somerset Maugham really was a spy.

● Somerset Maugham

Maugham was British, but he was born in Paris. When he was very young, he learned to speak English, French and German. He was so good at languages that Britain's spy department sent him to be a spy in Geneva, in Switzerland.

In Switzerland, Maugham pretended to be a French writer. He collected information from other spies about the German army and sent it back to England. The information was hidden in code in Maugham's handwritten books, so the Swiss police never looked at them too carefully.

After World War 1, Maugham wrote stories about his spy experiences. But he had to burn most of them because they contained too much secret information. In 1928, though, he did write a book about his work as a spy in St Petersburg, Russia. The name of one of the people in the book was *Somerville*. This was the name Maugham used when he worked in Russia as a spy for the British government in 1917.

● *Johnny Got His Gun*

Not all stories with codes and ciphers are about crimes and spies. In 1939, Dalton Trumbo wrote a book about an American soldier in World War 1 who loses both arms and both legs and the ability to see, speak or hear. He eventually uses Morse code to tell his story by hitting his head on his pillow. Trumbo hated war and wrote the book for people who thought that war was exciting.

● Dan Brown and *The Da Vinci Code*

One of the most popular books in the world today is a story about secret ciphers and codes. Dan Brown's *The Da Vinci Code* has been translated into forty-four languages. It begins with a murder at the Louvre, in Paris. There are strange symbols around the body, which the dead man wrote himself in his own blood. A man with a specialist interest in symbols and the dead man's granddaughter, a specialist in ciphers, see them. Together, they follow a number of clues. Many of the clues are connected with Leonardo da Vinci, an artist and inventor who lived in Italy five hundred years ago.

On the cover of *The Da Vinci Code*, there are other clues. These clues have no relationship with *The Da Vinci Code*, but are connected with the subject of Brown's next book. Thousands of readers followed the clues and were able to

Tom Hanks as Robert Langdon in The Da Vinci Code

solve the puzzle. The clues led them to a piece of art at the American spy department, the CIA. The work of art is called Kryptos. It is a large public cipher puzzle with letters cut out of metal.

The Da Vinci Code mixes fact and fiction. One fact is Brown's description of a tube-shaped container with disks that need to be lined up in the right order. If they are not, or if the tube is broken, a bottle of liquid inside will break and destroy the message. Leonardo da Vinci invented this cipher tube.

CHAPTER 8

Mountain Fires to Enigma

British scientists could not discover a way to break the code. Finally,
they found the reason …

It has always been difficult to send secret information over great distances.
When the Greeks celebrated the fall of the city of Troy in 1084 BC*, they
immediately wanted to tell their queen, Clytemnestra, the good news. She was
800 kilometres away in Mycenae, a two-day journey by horse or a five-day run.
Instead, the Greeks used signal fires. The first fire was lit and then another, 70
kilometres away, as waiting soldiers saw the signal. Each fire was lit in turn.
Twelve signal fires brought Clytemnestra the good news in a few minutes.

For hundreds of years, fires on the tops of mountains were probably the
fastest and easiest way to send a message across a great distance. But very little
information could be sent this way; usually just a warning or news that was
expected. Also, there were disadvantages; heavy rains or cloudy weather could
make the fires less easy to see. If the soldiers on the mountains were not paying
attention, they could miss a message.

● Other places, other ways

People in different parts of the world found other ways to send messages
– smoke signals, for example. Native Americans built a fire and used a blanket
to send up small clouds of smoke. Friends saw the patterns of smoke and
understood the code, but other people might just think that it was a fire. These
signals were not an effective way of sharing information. Part of the message – or
the *whole* message – might not be seen in time. Like mountaintop fires, smoke
signals might not be seen during bad weather; they were also useless at night.

In parts of Africa, drums were used to send messages, especially in places
where you could not see mountains or smoke. People could beat drums in
different ways, so drums could share more information than mountaintop fires.
Drums were also better because people noticed the sound of drums without
looking in their direction. But when enemies heard drumming, they could drum
too, and the noise could make the first message impossible to understand.

● Mechanical semaphore

In the late 1700s, a new idea became popular in France. It was a mechanical
semaphore similar to semaphore signals used over short distances by soldiers.

* BC: years before the birth of Christ

A semaphore station

Claude Chappe and his three brothers did not have jobs and were looking for a way to make money. They decided to build mechanical semaphore stations to send messages from one end of France to the other. At first, the brothers tried to use large squares of metal that looked like normal semaphore flags, but these metal flags were not easy to see over great distances. Instead, the Chappe brothers connected two large metal arms to a cross-arm. The two metal arms had seven positions each and the cross-arm had four positions. Together, they could offer a total of 196 symbols, including letters, numbers and special symbols in code.

The brothers built several lines of stations across France. Each station was on a hilltop twelve to twenty-five kilometres from the next one. There were, for example, fifteen stations in the 240 kilometres between Paris and Lille. A fifty-letter message could be sent in an hour.

The Chappe brothers' invention was soon popular not just in France, but all around Europe. But it still had a few problems. The stations were hard to see in bad weather and, although the Chappes tried fixing lights to the arms, the lights could not be seen clearly at night. Messages could be sent in code. But everyone could see Chappe's semaphore stations, so it was possible that someone could break a code and learn a secret. Few business people wanted to use the stations. Finally, another invention took the place of the Chappes' semaphore stations. The inventor was a young American artist named Samuel Morse.

● Morse code

Morse studied drawing and painting, but he was also interested in electricity and inventions. On an 1832 boat trip from London to New York, he heard some people talking about electrical **magnets**. He decided he could use electrical magnets to send messages over great distances. An electrical signal could turn a magnet at the other end of a line on and off.

Morse worked on his invention for six years. In 1838, he finally showed the world a **telegraph** that could send a message in a code of short and long sounds. This code could be sent on an electrical line, read at the other end and turned back into words. Interest was slow at first but then Morse, and several companies, built long-distance lines to carry news around the United States.

A telegraph machine

Although it was very convenient that messages could be printed out on paper, trained Morse operators could receive fifty words a minute by ear. Morse code telegraph messages could be sent day or night over any distance. There was one problem: telegraph lines could be cut or knocked down in a storm. But people still learn Morse code because it can be sent with mirrors, lights or bells. The most famous Morse code signal is SOS, the signal for Help!: ... --- ...

magnet /ˈmægnət/ (n) a piece of metal that makes other metal things move towards it
telegraph /ˈteləgrɑːf/ (n) an old-fashioned way of sending messages using electrical signals

● Secrets by radio

The invention of radio allowed people to send secret messages through the air. Even after radio became used more than telegraph lines, Morse code was still popular. But anyone with a radio could listen to the messages, so radio messages were often sent in code. This was especially true during times of war, but also for normal business secrets. For example, banks frequently sent secret messages to their offices around the world.

Governments and businesses were always trying to break each other's secret codes. Most early codes were not too difficult if you were clever and had some skills in mathematics. But in 1933, the British government began noticing strange secret Morse code messages from Germany. British scientists could not discover a way to break the cipher. Finally, they found the reason: these new messages were made using a new cipher machine called Enigma, invented by the German inventor Arthur Scherbius.

At first, Scherbius sold the Enigma to German companies, but the German government soon took an interest in Enigma's ability to offer 'unbreakable' codes.

The machine itself looked like a box with keys and several disks that turned around each time a new letter was pressed. The Enigma's disks could be changed and the machine could mix every single letter of a message into a new and different cipher.

When World War 2 began in 1939, Germany used the Enigma machine to communicate with its ships and submarines as well as with its armies abroad. Enigma operators used secret codebooks to broadcast their Enigma messages each day. The Germans broke other countries' codes and ciphers and used the information to attack planes and ships in the Atlantic Ocean. Someone needed to break the Enigma cipher!

● Breaking Enigma

Before World War 2, Polish mathematicians were able to steal a German Enigma machine and began to understand how it worked. But the Germans then added more disks and made the code more difficult. Suddenly, Enigma could send a coded message in 159,000,000,000,000,000,000 ways!

The British government hired many of England's top scientists and mathematicians – and many people who were simply good at word games and finding solutions to puzzles. They were sent to break the Enigma cipher at Bletchley Park, a private home with large grounds outside London. Bletchley Park soon became the centre of British code-breaking activities. Every day, thousands of enemy messages were collected and sent there for people to work on. Among these code-breakers was the young mathematician Alan Turing.

Turing had two important ideas that helped to break Enigma. He learned that no letter could ever be a code for itself; a ciphered *A* could not be an *A*. He also learned that at 6:05 each morning, when German ships and submarines sent their weather reports using Enigma, they often used similar words, like times, dates and the German word for 'weather'.

To save time, Turing invented an early computer which matched coded messages to real words. Turing's computer and codebooks from a sinking German submarine helped the

An Enigma machine

British solve the Enigma ciphers and read all secret German messages.

Of course, the British government did not tell the German government this! Instead, they used the information to stop German attacks on their ships and to attack German ships, planes and submarines. The British sent messages about each success in a radio cipher that they knew the Germans could understand, pretending that their successes were the results of luck. The Germans believed in Enigma and did not guess the true situation. Many people think that Britain's use of the Enigma ciphers helped win the war.

● The last Enigma secret

Sadly, after the war, the British government still thought that Enigma should be a secret. They could not afford to share their knowledge because Germany or another country might try to use a machine like Enigma again. The decipherers of the Enigma code were not allowed to talk about the work. Most of them died before their families and friends learnt that they were heroes.

5.1 **Were you right?**

Look back at Activity 4.4. Were your stories described in these chapters? Then match these clues to the stories on the right.

1   a light in the window · · · · · · · · · ·   **a**   *Johnny Got His Gun*

2   seeds in a letter   **b**   'The Adventure of the Jumping Men'

3   an old document   **c**   'The Adventure of the Red Circle'

4   every third word   **d**   'The Five Orange Pips'

5   drawings outside a house   **e**   'The Gloria Scott'

6   hidden writing   **f**   'The Gold Bug'

7   Morse code   **g**   'The Musgrave Ritual'

5.2 **What more did you learn?**

Write notes about the advantages and disadvantages of these methods of sending messages.

	Advantages	Disadvantages
Signal fires		
Drums		
Mechanical semaphore		
Morse code		
Radio		
Enigma machine		

5.3 Language in use

Use the punctuation marks in the box to correct these sentences from Chapters 7 and 8.

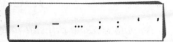

1 Conan Doyle who wrote the Sherlock Holmes stories was a doctor
   not a detective he started writing detective stories because not
   enough sick people came to see him and he needed another way to make money

2 It is finally found but looks unimportant a bag of old metal and stones

3 It means Come here at once

4 One light means *a* two lights mean *b* three lights mean *c*

5 Part of the message or the *whole* message might not be seen in time

5.4 What's next?

Chapter 9 is called 'Speaking in Code'. Do you know any ways of *speaking* so that other people do not understand? Talk to other students and make notes here.

Notes

Speaking in Code

Navajo is also a difficult language to speak. Some sounds in the language are not said through the mouth – they are only made through the nose.

P arents often want to say things that they do not want their children to understand. They might use long words or speak in another language – until their children learn that language.

● Cockney

English speakers sometimes use an invented language when they do not know another language. Criminals in England learnt to say words backwards so police and other people could not understand them easily.

Speakers of Cockney, a form of English, use many words that sound like other words. *Boat race*, for example, means *face* – but Cockney speakers use a short form and just say, 'I like your boat.' In Cockney, the words *dog and bone* mean *telephone* and a Cockney speaker might say, 'I'm on the dog.' The meaning is very difficult to guess for someone who does not understand Cockney. Also, Cockney is always changing. It often uses the names of famous people for new words, so the words change as different people become famous.

● Pig Latin

A different kind of code is Pig Latin. You can speak Pig Latin by changing the order of letters in English words and adding some letters, such as *ay* or *yay*. People speak it in different ways, but here are the two most common rules:

1. If a word begins with *a, e, i, o, u* or *y*, add *yay* to the end of the word.
   a = *ayay*
   am = *amyay*
   I = *iyay*
   in = *inyay*
   you = *youyay*

2. If it does not, take away all the letters before the *a, e, i, o, u* or *y* and put them at the end of the word, followed by *ay*.
   big = *igbay*
   Latin = *atinlay*
   listen = *istenlay*
   pig = *igpay*
   secret = *ecretsay*
   telling = *ellingtay*

You can put these words together to say, *istenlay iyay amyay ellingtay youyay ayay igbay ecretsay inyay igpay atinlay:* 'Listen, I am telling you a big secret in Pig Latin.'

Another code like this places *ab* before each of the letters *a, e, i, o, u* and *y* in a word. A sentence like *I already know that secret.* becomes *abi abalrabeabadaby knabow thabat sabecrabet* It sounds difficult but, with practice, you can do it!

Pig Latin and similar codes are really only used for speaking. If you write messages in those codes, they are easy to decipher.

● Wind Talkers

Time is important for many secret codes and ciphers. With enough time, a scientist or a spy can break almost any secret code using a computer. So it is important to send messages that take a long time to break. By the time your enemy has decoded the message, it is probably no longer important.

Spoken secret codes and ciphers need to be remembered by the people who use them, so a lot of training is necessary. But a little-known language can be a useful code and it can be easy to find speakers of the language who learned it as children. They do not need as much training.

Philip Johnston had a special skill and an unusual idea. In 1942, the United States was in the middle of World War 2. In Europe, Africa and the Atlantic Ocean, Americans were fighting Germans. In Asia and the Pacific Ocean, the Americans were fighting the Japanese. Johnston remembered that in World War 1, seventeen years earlier, Chocataw Native Americans had used their language on the radio to confuse German soldiers. Johnston realised that Native American languages could be a good way to send coded messages. More important, he knew a lot about one Native American language: Navajo (said /'nævəhəʊ/).

Johnston's father had lived and worked with Navajo Native Americans in the American Southwest, and Johnston had grown up with Navajo children. As he played with them, he naturally started to learn their language and customs. In all, he lived among the Navajo for twenty-four years.

Johnston did not just know how to speak the Navajo language; he also knew a lot about it. For example, he knew that it was *only* a spoken language. There were no letters, symbols or written words in Navajo. Because of this, there was no dictionary. Few people in the world had ever studied Navajo. This meant that there were no written descriptions of how the language worked and no easy way for people to learn it. Only the Navajo people themselves, Johnston, and about twenty other people could speak or understand the Navajo language. Most importantly, German and Japanese enemies were very unlikely to speak it.

Navajo is a very difficult language to learn. It is quite unlike other languages. To speak the language, you need to understand how a Navajo thinks. For example, an English-speaking person may say 'I am hungry', but a Navajo will translate the idea as 'Hunger is hurting me.'

Navajo is also a difficult language to speak. Some sounds in the language are not said through the mouth – they are only made through the nose. Words change meaning if they are said softly or loudly, or with a movement of the voice up or down. If you do not understand how the language works, you can hear similar sounds repeated many times and not understand that they are different words.

● Into the army

In early 1942, Johnston went to his local army centre and asked to speak to Clayton P. Vogel. Vogel was a top officer in the United States Army. Secret codes were important to him and to American soldiers to plan their attacks and also to call for help when they needed it. But it could be more dangerous if an enemy heard and understood a message. They needed a quick way to send messages that could not be easily understood. Often, these messages needed to be sent in difficult and dangerous conditions.

Johnston explained his idea. Navajo soldiers could translate an English message and say it over the radio in Navajo. A Navajo speaker would listen on another radio and translate the message back into English.

In February, 1942, Johnston brought five Navajo speakers together to meet Vogel. Vogel gave them a test to see how the method could work. Half of the Navajo were given messages in English. At the same time, soldiers shouted and made lots of noise with guns to copy war conditions. Other Navajo speakers received the messages and translated them back into English. The test worked perfectly. The translated messages were exactly the same as the ones that were sent.

Later that year, Vogel started a special army training camp for the first twenty-nine Navajo Native Americans code speakers. They called themselves Wind Talkers. The Wind Talkers first had to learn about being soldiers. Next they had to learn about sending and receiving secret codes. The Navajo language covered many important words like colours, but it did not cover special army terms for different kinds of guns, bombs, boats, aeroplanes and land vehicles. The first Navajo Wind Talkers developed code words for these terms. Many of the aeroplanes were named after birds and many of the boats were named after fish.

Place names also needed code words. The United States was called *our mother*, the islands of Britain were called *land between waters* and Spain was called *sheep pain.* If you say *sheep pain* quickly, it sounds like *shpain,* close to the sound of *Spain.*

● New words

The Wind Talkers developed more than six hundred terms to describe different things, but they were not enough. Sometimes they had to spell the name of a special place or a person. But if they used one group of words for the letters, the enemy might start to understand the cipher, so for most letters the Navajo Wind Talkers used three different Navajo words, changing them often. For example, the letter *H* was ciphered as *tse-gah* (hair), *cha* (hat) or *lin* (horse). Of course it was necessary to keep everything secret, so no written copies of the code were allowed outside the training camps. The Navajo Wind Talkers had to remember everything.

To test the new code and cipher, the army found Navajo speakers who did not work for the army. These other speakers of the Navajo language could not guess the meaning of the coded and ciphered messages. This meant that the test was a success.

A Navajo Wind Talker

By 1945, more than four hundred Navajo Wind Talkers were sending thousands of messages. Most importantly, the Navajo Wind Talker code was never broken and the Navajo Wind Talkers helped the United States to win World War 2.

● For women only!

For about 1,700 years, girls and women in Pumei Village, in southern China, used a secret language that was never shared with men or boys. The name of the language is Nashu. Today, only about ten people know how to speak it.

Boys and men learned to read and write Chinese but girls did not learn; until recently, they did not go to school at all. Instead, girls in Pumei Village taught themselves to read and write their own secret language.

Nashu started as a way for young girls and women to make friends and share secrets. The written form of Nashu is quite different from written Chinese. Some of the symbols look like Chinese symbols, but each one is a letter, not a word, so it is easier to learn.

Older women first taught younger girls Nashu by singing songs in the secret language and then talking and telling stories in it. Girls were then taught how to write the language. Often, they did not have paper to write on. They wrote on their hands to practise. Sometimes they wrote a message on a handkerchief as a gift to another woman.

When a girl married, she left her friends and went to live with her husband. The third day after she was married, friends gave her a special book. The first few pages of the book were written in Nashu by female friends and relatives. The rest of the pages of the book were empty pages for the young woman to write a diary in Nashu. Chinese girls now learn to read and write in school and do not need to read and write in a secret language. Nashu is a dying language.

CHAPTER 10

Talking with Your Body

Hand signals are important when people cannot hear each other
or do not want to be heard.

C an you recognise whether a stranger is happy or unhappy? There is one secret language that everyone speaks but not everyone understands: body language. Body language is all the communication in a conversation except the actual words you use. There are two different kinds of body language: body language that we can control and body language that we cannot control.

● Uncontrolled body language

We are born with body language that we cannot control. It shows how we feel. For example, blind children do not *learn* to smile by seeing someone else smile. Although they never see anyone smile, they still do it. All humans smile. In the same way, deaf children laugh, although they never hear anyone else laughing.

It is easiest to read the body language of children. When they are tired, sad or happy, their bodies show it immediately. As children get older, they try to control their body language. Adults control theirs for many reasons. They may not want other people to think they are afraid when they speak in front of a group. They may not want to show that they are bored because they want to be polite. But people cannot always control themselves.

The human body has many ways to give messages about how we feel. Many of these messages come from emotions like boredom, anger and jealousy. Often, our body's messages are not the same as the ones we give through our speech. We may give a polite 'yes' while showing with a shake of our head and crossed arms our true feelings: 'no'.

These messages teach us a lot about what people really mean. Sometimes, they also help us understand when other people are lying, because their words do not match their body language. But body language is different all around the world. How many of the kinds of body language shown on the next page do you use? Do they have the same meaning?

● Body language you control

The second kind of body language is the kind we can control. We may smile when we are happy, but a smile can also give other kinds of messages. It may show that we believe something, or that we agree. It may let someone know that they are doing a good job. And we use many different kinds of smile to greet someone or to call attention to ourselves in a shop or restaurant.

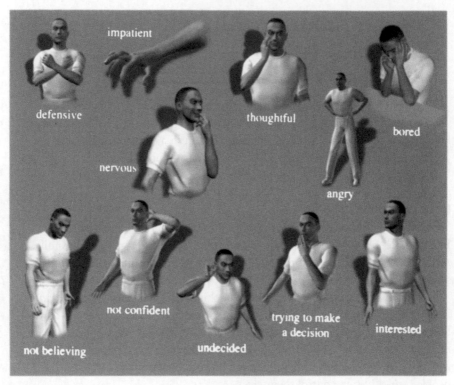

Body language

But people do not just smile with their lips; we use our whole face to show real pleasure. The lines around our eyes move too. People sometimes smile with their lips but not with their eyes when they are just being polite.

People use body language to give many kinds of orders. A police officer uses body language to give directions to traffic. Sports teams use body language to tell team members how to play. They can use hand signals that the other team cannot understand.

In Hong Kong, jewellery traders discuss the price of special jewels or stones by putting their hands under a newspaper or blanket. They pull on each other's fingers to agree a price and use code words to say if the price is in the hundreds or thousands.

Hand signals are important when people cannot hear each other or do not want to be heard. Police and soldiers use hand signals to give secret commands. Small radios have made some of these signals less important, but one group of people still uses hand signals every day: the deaf.

Martha's Vineyard is an island on the east coast of the United States. For almost two hundred years there was a small population on the island and people often married within the same families. But many of these people had a medical problem that made them and their children deaf. By the late 1800s there were twenty times as many deaf people on Martha's Vineyard as in most other places in the world.

These deaf people had no problem communicating. They developed their own sign language for everyday use and most people on Martha's Vineyard used it. Even hearing people used it to communicate with other hearing people. Children learnt it to communicate behind their teachers' backs in class.

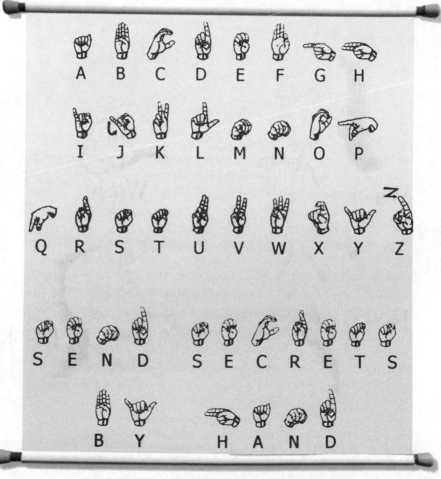

American Sign Language

In 1817, after learning sign language in France, a group of teachers opened a school for the deaf in Hartford, Connecticut in the United States. Many deaf students from Martha's Vineyard went there to learn, but they also took their own sign language with them. The two languages mixed and the new language was soon called American Sign Language.

American sign language has two parts: body language symbols, which are like a code, and alphabet symbols that are like a cipher. Some signs are easy to understand, like pointing to yourself with the first finger of your right hand to show *I*, or using your open right hand to show *my*. Some other signs are easy to understand when they are explained; the use of your right hand to brush pretend snow off your left shoulder means *Canadian*. Other signs just need to be memorised.

American Sign Language

But although American Sign Language is used everywhere in North America, people in other English-speaking countries like Britain do not understand it. They use their own signs. There is no international sign language.

Children and animals

At what age can someone start to learn sign language? Babies cannot talk before a certain age – their mouths, throats and tongues are not ready. But in the 1980s, a university student noticed his deaf friends communicating with their babies in sign. The man found that these babies learn to communicate with their parents much earlier than hearing children. They use simple hand signs for things that they wanted to have or do.

The man's own child was not deaf, but he tried it. He found that the baby could quickly learn to make simple signs. Now many people use sign language with their hearing babies. The signs are for things like hat, toy, milk, sleep and food.

Animals cannot talk for the same reason that babies cannot. Their mouths, throats and tongues are not the right shapes. Also, many animals do not have lips. Scientists wondered if animals could learn to use signs to explain what they wanted. There have been many tests. Some scientists say the tests prove animals can learn to speak in signs. But other people disagree and say the scientists have not proved anything.

Secret handshakes

The Masons, also called the Freemasons, are part of a large international group of men who like to share secrets, help each other and help others. The Masons is an old organisation. It started around the 1700s and perhaps as early as four hundred years earlier. Masons give themselves special names and greet each other with secret signals and handshakes.

6.1 Were you right?

Look back at Activity 5.4. Then answer these questions.

1 Write your name in Pig Latin. (Mine is *enkay eattybay*)

....

2 What does the Cockney sentence 'I'm on the dog.' mean?

....

3 Make up a new word or sentence in Cockney.

....

4 Write your name in the ab code.

....

5 What are the names of America and Spain in Navajo Wind Talker code?

....

6 What is Nashu?

....

6.2 What more did you learn?

Circle T for true and F for false.

1	Blind children learn to smile by listening.	T	F
2	All body language is uncontrolled.	T	F
3	American Sign Language is uncontrolled body language.	T	F
4	One sign of nervousness is biting your fingers.	T	F
5	Some people drum their fingers to show impatience.	T	F
6	Hearing babies cannot learn sign language.	T	F
7	Some hearing people speak to each other in sign language.	T	F

6.3 Language in use

Look at the sentences in the box.
What is the difference in meaning?
Add commas to these sentences if
they need them.

> The army found Navajo **speakers
> who** did not work for the army.
> The army found Navajo **speakers,
> who** did not work for the army.

1 Cockneys who speak a form of English are difficult to understand.

2 Cockneys speak a form of English that is always changing.

3 Do you know anyone who can speak Pig Latin?

4 Johnston spoke Navajo which gave him a good idea.

5 The girls in Pumei Village who could not write Chinese wrote in a secret language.

6 American Sign Language is a language which deaf people use.

6.4 What's next?

Do you recognise this stone,
or can you guess what it is?
Discuss why it might
be important.

CHAPTER 11

Lost Words

He decided to discover the meaning of hieroglyphics and spent the next eighteen years studying them.

A ll languages are secret codes for people who cannot understand them. In most cases, it is easy to learn other languages; there is no reason for them to be secret at all. You can go to the library or take classes or visit another country and learn. But some languages are simply lost. The speakers and writers of those languages have all died and there is no record of how the languages sounded or what the writings mean.

● Egyptian hieroglyphics

One of the oldest and most famous of these languages is Egyptian **hieroglyphics**. Hieroglyphics is an unusual kind of writing. It includes 6,000 different symbols. Some symbols are quite simple: a picture of a knife means *knife* or *cut*. Some are detailed pictures of gods, people and animals. But for 1,400 years, no one could begin to guess how to read these strange symbols or even what they sounded like.

After 1798, this situation changed. The French leader Napoleon Bonaparte took his army to Egypt. He also took 167 scientists with him. The scientists wanted to study Egypt's art and old buildings and to try to understand Egypt's past and its language.

Later that year, soldiers found a large piece of black stone near the Egyptian town of Rosetta. The 762-kilogram stone was part of a building that the soldiers were taking down. On the stone was a message in three languages, including hieroglyphics. The scientists quickly decided that the stone was the clue they were looking for. If they could understand one of the languages, they might be able to understand hieroglyphics.

One of the languages was easy to understand. It was old Greek. Scientists soon understood the message. It written in 196 BC and talked about the new leader of Egypt, a thirteen year-old boy named Ptolemy V Epiphanes. The other language was Demotic. Demotic is old Egyptian writing that is simpler to read and write than hieroglyphics. But it was still not understood.

The French scientists made paper copies of the Rosetta Stone's writings and sent them to other scientists in Europe. But many years passed before anyone could understand how to read hieroglyphics. The answer did not come from a

hieroglyphics /ˌhaɪrəˈɡlɪfɪks/ (n) a way of writing that uses pictures instead of words. A *glyph* is a symbol, usually a picture, that gives information.

The Rosetta Stone

famous scientist; a young Frenchman, Jean François Champollion, discovered the secret.

As a young boy, Champollion was very interested in languages. He learned Arabic, Chinese, Chaldean, Hebrew and Syriac. He later learned Coptic, Ethiopic, Sanskrit, Zend, Pahlevi and Persian. All these languages helped him to understand how a lost language like Egyptian hieroglyphics might work.

One day, a famous scientist came to his school. The scientist had visited Egypt and Champollion had learned everything he could about Egypt. He had many questions for the scientist. Finally, the scientist laughed: 'Who went to Egypt? You or me?' The scientist thought that Champollion was a great student and later helped him study at a better school.

When Champollion was eighteen years old, he saw a copy of the Rosetta Stone. He decided to discover the meaning of hieroglyphics and spent the next eighteen years studying them. People had different ideas about what hieroglyphics might mean. Some people thought each symbol was a different word. Some people thought that the symbols were only pretty pictures – decorations. Some thought that the different symbols were letters of an Egyptian alphabet.

Another problem was the direction of the sentences. The sentences sometimes went from left to right and sometimes from right to left, but there was one clue: the animal heads always faced the start of each sentence.

Champollion knew that written Hebrew and Arabic texts do not include the *a, e, i, o* or *u* sounds. Sometimes they are also not included in written English. For example, we write the short form *Rd* for *road*. But it would be confusing if we shortened every word in this way. Two letters like *bt* could represent a number of words, including *beat, boat* and *boot*.

Champollion decided that hieroglyphics worked the same way but that they used a symbol at the start of the sentence to explain what it was about. For example, if the *bt* word was *boat*, the first symbol might be about *water*.

Champollion thought about these different ideas and looked at more and more examples of hieroglyphics. He found that sometimes symbols were in a little box. Champollion guessed that these symbols might stand for the name of a king or queen.

Egyptian hieroglyphics

Champollion found characters in the boxes that represented the sounds for *RMSS* and *KLPDR*. When he guessed the other letters, he had the names of an Egyptian king and queen: *Ramses* and *Kliopadra* (Cleopatra). This told Champollion that Egyptian hieroglyphics were made up of sounds, and were not just pictures of ideas.

Champollion jumped up from his desk and ran across town to see his brother. 'I have done it!' he shouted. Then he fell down and did not get out of bed for eight days. The lost language of the Egyptians could finally be read and heard again.

● Cuneiform

Cuneiform was another language that was lost for thousands of years. It was first used more than 5,000 years ago and was popular for about 3,000 years. It was used by the people who lived in the area around modern Iraq. These people did not use paper to write on. Instead, they used **clay**. If the message was not important, the clay could be put in water and used again. If the message was important, the clay could be baked hard. Then it lasted for centuries.

Often, clay messages were baked by accident. When an enemy army attacked, it often burned down a city. The clay messages in the houses and buildings were baked in the fires. After that, the messages might be buried in the desert sands for hundreds or thousands of years.

Cuneiform was written with a small pointed stick. A writer

Cuneiform

quickly made small marks in the wet clay. Like Egyptian hieroglyphics, cuneiform began as pictures of things that people wanted to buy and sell. The first pictures were of animals and food. A trader drew a picture of a cow on one clay disk and used it like money. If there were five cows, he made five clay disks. Later, cuneiform writers developed numbers. Instead of five disks for cows, the trader could use one disk for *cows* and one disk with the number *five* on it. Eventually, traders made one disk with the number five and a cow on it and the disks became coins.

These pictures became simpler as people had to write them faster. In time, it became very hard to recognise the old pictures.

clay /kleɪ/ (n) a type of heavy earth that is used for making pots and bricks

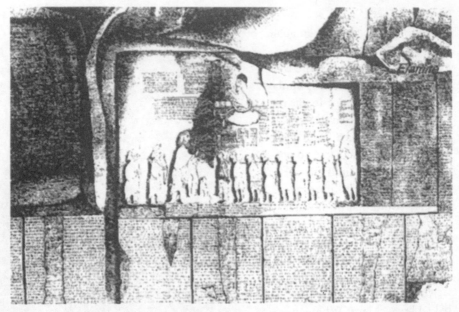

Writing in stone, in Behistun

Although it was an important language for 3,000 years, cuneiform became a lost language that no one could read. Then, in 1835, a British soldier, Henry Rawlinson, found some writing on a rock at Behistun in Persia (now in Iraq).

The writing had been cut into the stone during the time of King Darius I. He was the king of Persia from 522 to 486 BC. Like the Rosetta Stone, the same texts were written in three languages: Old Persian, Babylonian cuneiform and Elamite.

Rawlinson spoke Persian and was able to translate the least difficult text – old Persian – first. It told the story of King Darius. After that, Rawlinson began the hard work of deciphering the cuneiform. By 1851, he could read two hundred cuneiform signs. Cuneiform is no longer a lost language and we can understand a lot about daily life 2,500 years ago.

CHAPTER 12

Human Nature

In the history of secret codes and ciphers, people have often missed finding clues or solving problems for personal reasons.

Ciphers and codes are only as good as the people who use them. They have been broken because people have been careless or because spies have been clever. Mata Hari was a Dutch spy who worked for the Germans during World War 1. But she made a mistake and sent information to them using an old cipher. The French were able to understand the message, so the Germans were angry and punished her. They sent her a message in another cipher that they knew the French could read. The message gave away Mata Hari's name. The French government found and shot her.

● Stealing secrets

Thieves find it easy to steal information from people's computers or banks because people are less careful about their secret codes than they are about the locks on their doors. For example, many people write down their code words and keep them in their wallets or on their desks.

In other cases, thieves use 'social engineering'; they use people's foolishness and fears to get the secrets they want. For example, a thief may telephone you and say there is a problem with your computer or bank. If you agree to give them your secret word or other information, you can lose a lot of money quickly and easily. Thieves even go through people's rubbish to look for letters from banks or information about bank cards. People are now more careful with information about their secret codes and bank information, but thieves still find new ways to steal what they want.

● Mistakes

In the history of secret codes and ciphers, people have often missed finding clues or solving problems for personal reasons. In the 1920s, the Americans learned about Japanese codes by breaking into their government office in New York and photographing their codebook. During World War 2, Germans used the effective Enigma cipher to keep their secrets, but they shared their plans with Japanese officials and politicians who then talked about the German plans. Because the British and Americans could break the less difficult Japanese codes and ciphers, they had a better idea of what the Germans were doing.

Human nature means that people make mistakes for many reasons – or they may be punished for their success. Joseph J Rochefort was the World War 2 cipher breaker who thought the Japanese were going to attack Midway Island. His boss thought that they were going to attack Alaska. Rochefort was right and found a way to prove it by sending a false message. But his boss was jealous and Rochefort never worked in codes and ciphers again.

● The Mayan Glyphs

In the 16th and 17th centuries, Spanish soldiers went to the 'New World' for gold. They found it in the area of Mexico and Central America. They took guns, the Christian religion and disease with them. The Mayan people tried to fight against the Spanish, but they were not strong enough.

The Spanish found a rich society. Mayans had built great cities and developed a written language around 100 BC. These cities lasted until the Spanish arrived. The Mayan people had beautiful art and great writings which told their history and their stories. They also had beautiful writing – among the most beautiful in the world. But it was almost completely lost.

Mayan glyphs

Other languages, like Egyptian hieroglyphics, were lost because people just stopped using them. But Mayan glyphs were lost because the Spanish did not like them. One man especially wanted to get rid of them: a religious leader called Diego de Landa.

De Landa hated Mayan glyphs. He wanted to bring the Christian religion to the people of the Americas. He did not understand the glyphs and thought that their pictures of Mayan gods would stop the Mayan people from accepting Christianity. He ordered the Spanish soldiers to destroy all Mayan books and pictures. No one knows how many books were burned, but we do know that only three are left today.

Mayan writing has hundreds of different signs, or glyphs, in the form of humans, animals, gods and everyday tools.

De Landa destroyed much of Mayan language and art, but he also helped to save it. In 1566, he wrote a book about his time in Latin America and thought he should say something about the language. He decided to ask some of the Mayan people to write down their alphabet.

In fact, the Mayans did not have an alphabet. They simply wrote the pictures that they used for each of the sounds that he said. If someone asked you for the picture for the English letter *c*, you might misunderstand and draw a *sea*.

Slowly, the Mayan language was lost. But fortunately, it was not just kept in books. The Mayan people left their writing on stone buildings. Many foreigners knew that there were lost cities in Central America and two travellers, John Lloyd Stephens and Frederick Catherwood, visited some of them in 1839. Catherwood made drawings and paintings of the ruins they found and people became very interested in Mayan writing. In the 1920s, John Eric Thompson collected and organised thousands of Mayan symbols.

Thompson was a specialist in the Mayan symbols, but he had his own ideas about what they meant. He fought with anyone who disagreed. Some people think that his ideas slowed learning about Mayan writing for forty years. The Russian scientist Yuri Knorosov finally found a way to read the Mayan texts using de Landa's alphabet writing. For a long time, Thompson and the Americans did not believe him simply because they did not like Russians.

● The largest codes

Is there intelligent life in other worlds? Are there living beings like people or are they completely different? If they are, what are they like? What will they say to us? These are questions that scientists have tried to answer for more than forty years.

In 1959, two scientists at Cornell University explained how radio waves could be sent between the stars. This made people think. Were there scientific societies in other worlds sending radio messages?

In 1960, a scientist called Frank Drake used a radio telescope to listen for signs from another world. He listened for several weeks. He did not find anything, but others were interested in the idea. More and more scientists began looking for life among the stars. One group uses people's home computers to help examine information collected by radio telescopes. When you are not working on your computer, a program can use it to look for signals that could be messages. Other scientists send out messages for people from other worlds to hear.

What do scientists expect to find? People from another world are not likely to speak English or any other known language. They may send out radio waves. If the signals are regular and repeated, we will know that someone from another world is trying to communicate.

In addition to radio wave signals, scientists on Earth have tried to send another kind of code on a space ship.

The Voyager space ship message is on a thirty-centimetre metal disk. The disk contains sounds and pictures that show different kinds of life on Earth. There are 115 pictures and many sounds from nature. These include sounds of the ocean, different kinds of weather, birds and other animals. There is music from different countries and from

A radio telescope in the UK

different times through history. There are also greetings in fifty-five languages. Some of the languages are 6,000 years old. But you should not expect to hear from another world too soon. It will take 40,000 years for Voyager to get close to another world that might contain life.

By then, perhaps no one will remember the message that we sent or the languages that we now speak. Will we use our intelligence to fight wars or make friends? The important question is whether human nature will make people want to keep secrets or share ideas.

The history of secret codes and ciphers shows how clever people can be – at making secret codes and ciphers and at breaking them. It is unlikely that anyone will ever develop the perfect secret code or cipher that no one can break. It may take a long time and be very difficult, but it will be broken. Everyone likes to know a secret.

1 **Work in small groups. Every secret code and cipher has its advantages, but also its disadvantages.**

  a Each student should choose a different code or cipher and make notes on its strengths and weaknesses.

Notes

  b Now discuss the different codes and ciphers with the other people in your group. Which is the best? Vote to decide.

2 **Work in small groups. There are many fictional and real characters in this book.**

  a Discuss which one you would most like to be, and why.

  b Which character would be a good spy if they were alive now? Choose one character each and make notes here.

  c Discuss which of those people would make the best spy. Vote to decide.

Notes

Write a story that includes the use of secret codes and ciphers. Start with the sentence below and use all these words in your story.

body language	clue	decipher	email	puzzle
	represent	signal	translate	

I had heard stories about modern slavery, but

1 **Work in groups of three.**

You are in your house with two friends one night. Suddenly, a gang of thieves break down the door and lock you in a room. They want to steal everything in the house, but they also want to kidnap the three of you! They hope to get money from your families. You can hear them talking. One says that they are going to take you to a hut by a lake. Soon they are going to tie you up and put you in their car.

Your brother is arriving at the house in an hour. Quick! Talk to your two friends and decide how you can leave a secret message for your brother and the police. The kidnappers must not find it!

Notes

2 **Work in the same groups of three.**

You and your friends are now in the hut. You have a few minutes while the thieves are in the next room. You need to talk, but you want to talk in code. Write a list of the ten most important words or sentences that you might need to use to help you escape. Then think of easy-to-remember code words or a cipher that will help you share information.

Notes

3 **Work in the same groups.**

Two of you are locked in a room under the hut. Your friend is locked in the next room. Look around the room. What might you be able to use to make, send or hide secret messages? Can you send messages outside? Can you get a message to your friend in the next room? Remember that the thieves must not know what you are doing!

4 **It worked! You are free! The local newspaper has asked you to write your story.**

When the kidnappers arrived and locked us in a room, we were
surprised and frightened. We knew we had to think quickly. First, we